Biaozhun Jiaocheng
标准教程 2
STANDARD COURSE

主编　苏英霞
Lead Author Su Yingxia

编者　王蕾
Author Wang Lei

高等教育出版社 · 北京

《YCT标准教程》

总 策 划： 许　琳

总 监 制： 胡志平　　查卫平

监　　制： 段　莉　　贾巍巍　　李佩泽

执行策划： 梁　宇　　张慧君　　金飞飞　　李亚男

主　　编： 苏英霞

编　　者： 第1册　　王　蕾

第2册　　王　蕾

第3册　　王淑红　　郝　琳

第4册　　王淑红　　解　红

第5册　　王文龙　　王　蕾

第6册　　苏英霞　　王　蕾

Youth Chinese Test (YCT) is an international standardized test of Chinese proficiency, which evaluates the ability of primary school and middle school students whose mother tongue is not Chinese to use the Chinese language in their daily lives and study. With the principle of "combining testing and teaching", we take much pleasure in publishing this series of *YCT Standard Course*.

1. Target Readers

· Overseas primary school and middle school students who take Chinese as a selective course.

· Students who are going to take the YCT.

2. Correspondence Between Textbooks and YCT

Textbook	YCT	Vocabulary	Class Hours (For Reference)
Book 1	Level 1	80	35～45
Book 2	Level 2	150	35～45
Book 3	Level 3	300	50～60
Book 4			50～60
Book 5	Level 4	600	60～70
Book 6			60～70

3. Design

· It provides a scientific curriculum and effective teaching methods. The series is compiled in accordance with the acquisition and study rules of Chinese as a second language, with a careful consideration of the features of primary school and middle school students' cognitive development.

· It aims to stimulate students' multiple intelligence. The series employs various learning approaches including pictures, activities, exercises, songs and stories that center on the same topic so as to promote primary school and middle school students' multi-intellectual development.

· It combines testing and teaching. Based on the syllabus of YCT, the series accomplishes the goals of "stimulating teaching with testing" and "promoting learning with testing" through the design of appropriate teaching content and exercises.

4. Features

· A full coverage of YCT. On the basis of an overall and careful analysis of YCT syllabus and test papers, the series is organized with function as the prominent building blocks and grammar as the underlying building blocks, so as to fully cover YCT's vocabulary, grammar and function items. Each lesson is accompanied by a YCT model test page. Students should be able to pass the corresponding level of YCT after finishing each book.

· An integrated combination of function and fun. The series emphasizes on the authenticity of the scene design, the naturalness and usefulness of the language, as well as the interestingness of the content. At the same time, it takes a careful consideration of students' affection and attitude. Through texts, games, songs and stories, we hope the series is able to arise students' interest in learning and help them enjoy it as they learn.

· A variety of activities and exercises in each section. There are activities and exercises in each teaching section in this series in order to provide teaching clues and exercise options for teachers.

· Listening and speaking taking the lead and followed by reading and writing. The series follows the principle that students proceed with reading and writing after achieving the goal of listening and speaking. The first 4 books do not have any requirements on writing Chinese characters.

5. How to Use Book 2

YCT Standard Course (Book 2) is designed for entry level primary school and middle school students. The book has 12 lessons, covering 86 words, 23 grammar and function items of YCT level 2. Lessons 1–11 are teaching lessons while Lesson 12 is a revision lesson. The suggested class hours for each lesson are 3~4 hours.

Each lesson in Book 2 consists of Key sentences, Let's learn (new words), Let's read (texts), Activities and exercises, Songs, Mini stories and Model test page.

· Key sentences. Each lesson has 2 key sentences. The sentences are both important function items of the lesson and the clues for the key grammar points.

· Let's learn (new words). Each lesson has about 10 new words, with no more than 3 words that are not included in the syllabus (all marked with *). Most nouns appear in the form of pictures and are followed with Chinese characters, *Pinyin* and English translation. The other words are followed with Chinese characters, *Pinyin*, English translation and collocations or sample sentences.

· Let's read (texts). Each lesson has 2 texts, with each text containing 1~2 turns, which mainly come from sentences from previous YCT. Questions after the texts help teachers evaluate if students have fully understood the texts.

· Activities and exercises. The book has both traditional exercises such as filling in the blank and matching, and interactive activities or games. The alternative activities and exercises help the class achieve a balance between being dynamic and static.

· Songs. Each lesson contains a song related to the topic. Students can sing and dance at the same time, which helps to develop their multiple intelligence through a variety of stimulations.

· Mini stories. Each lesson provides an interesting mini story related to the topic. Students can act it out in groups after reading it.

· Model test page. Each lesson has a YCT model test page attached, which helps students familiarize themselves with the test and pass YCT successfully after finishing the book.

The Confucius Institute Headquarters, China Higher Education Press and Chinese Testing International (CTI) have offered tremendous support and guidance during the planning and compiling of the series. Domestic and foreign experts in related fields have also given us many valuable comments and suggestions. It is our sincere wish that the *YCT Standard Course* could open the doors of Chinese learning for overseas primary school and middle school students, and help them learn and grow up with ease and joy.

Scan the QR Code for more resources.

Authors

November, 2015

目录
Contents

热身

Warm-up

1 Let's get to know each other

	Nǐ jiào shénme? 你叫什么？	Nǐ duō dà? 你多大？	Nǐ shì nǎ guó rén? 你是哪国人？	Nǐ xǐhuan chī shénme? 你喜欢吃什么？
1				
2				

Talk with at least 2 classmates in Chinese. Start with “你好” and use the questions given to get familiar with them. Then introduce them to the whole class.

2 Let's review the words  00-01

  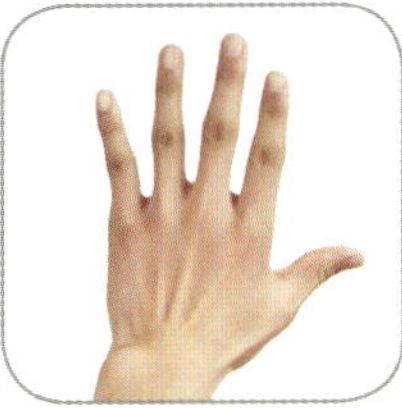   

Listen to the recording and tick the pictures. Try to find the pictures that are not included in the recording.

3 Let's find

zài 再	de 的	wǒ 我	lǎo 老	shī 师
hé 和	jiàn 见	men 们	hěn 很	xiǎo 小
shén 什	jīn 今	míng 明	niǎo 鸟	gè 个
xiàn 现	me 么	tiān 天	rèn 认	zi 子
bù 不	zài 在	jiā 家	dà 大	shí 识

Pair work. Try to find as many words and phrases as possible. Search the grid horizontally, vertically or diagonally.

4 Let's match

Jīntiān xīngqī jǐ? 今天星期几?	Tā bú zài. 他不在。
Nǐ bàba zài jiā ma? 你爸爸在家吗?	Wǒ yǒu liǎng ge jiějie. 我有两个姐姐。
Zhè shì nǐ de xiǎo māo ma? 这是你的小猫吗?	Jīntiān Xīngqītiān. 今天星期天。
Jīntiān jǐ yuè jǐ hào? 今天几月几号?	Wǒ chī píngguǒ. 我吃苹果。
Nǐ jiā yǒu jǐ kǒu rén? 你家有几口人?	Jīntiān èr yuè shí hào. 今天二月十号。
Nǐ chī shénme? 你吃什么?	Bú shì. 不是。
Nǐ yǒu jǐ ge jiějie? 你有几个姐姐?	Wǒ jiā yǒu wǔ kǒu rén. 我家有五口人。

Lesson 1

我可以坐这儿吗？

May I sit here?

Key Sentences

Wǒ kěyǐ zuò zhèr ma?
- 我可以坐这儿吗？ May I sit here?

Qǐng bú yào shuōhuà.
- 请 不要 说话。 Please be quiet.

kěyǐ 可以	may 不可以
zuò 坐	to sit 坐这儿
qǐng 请	please 请坐。
bú kèqi 不客气	You're welcome.
bú yào 不要	don't 请不要说话。
shuōhuà 说话	to talk, to speak 不说话
duìbuqǐ 对不起	I'm sorry.
méi guānxi 没关系	Never mind.

"N–1" game. The teacher says the new words a chosen number of times, and then the students repeat it one time less than the teacher.

Let's read

01-02

Question:他可以坐这儿吗？

Question:谁在说话？

Pair work. Read the dialogues and act them out.

Let's match

Lǎoshī hǎo. 老师好。	Bú kèqi. 不客气。
Xièxie. 谢谢。	Zàijiàn. 再见。
Duìbuqǐ. 对不起。	Nǐ hǎo. 你好。
Zàijiàn. 再见。	Méi guānxi. 没关系。

Let's play

Role play. Choose a picture, and then use Chinese to act it out with your partner.

Let's chant

Bàba, bàba, xièxie nín. Māma, māma, xièxie nín.
爸爸，爸爸，谢谢您。妈妈，妈妈，谢谢您。

Gēge, gēge, xièxie nǐ. Jiějie, jiějie, xièxie nǐ.
哥哥，哥哥，谢谢你。姐姐，姐姐，谢谢你。

Bú kèqi, bú kèqi.
不客气，不客气。

Bàba, bàba, duìbuqǐ. Māma, māma, duìbuqǐ.
爸爸，爸爸，对不起。妈妈，妈妈，对不起。

Gēge, gēge, duìbuqǐ. Jiějie, jiějie, duìbuqǐ.
哥哥，哥哥，对不起。姐姐，姐姐，对不起。

Méi guānxi, méi guānxi.
没关系，没关系。

Huīgūniang

灰姑娘

Do you know the end of the story? Ask your classmates and act out the whole story.

Test

1 Listening: True or false. 01-05

1.		
2.		
3.		
4.		

2 Reading.

Xièxie. 5. 谢谢。	☐	A	Bù, xièxie. 不，谢谢。
Nǐ hē shuǐ ma? 6. 你喝 水 吗？	☐	B	Kěyǐ, qǐng zuò. 可以，请 坐。
Qǐng bú yào shuōhuà. 7. 请 不要 说话。	☐	C	Bú kèqi. 不客气。
Nǐ hǎo, wǒ kěyǐ zuò zhèr ma? 8. 你好，我可以坐 这儿 吗？	☐	D	Hǎode, duìbuqǐ. 好的，对不起。

Lesson 2 你早上几点起床？

When do you get up in the morning?

Key Sentences

Wǒ zǎoshang qī diǎn qǐchuáng.
- 我 早上 七点 起床。 I get up at seven o'clock in the morning.

Jīntiān wǎnshang wǒ kěyǐ bú shuìjiào ma?
- 今天 晚上 我可以不睡觉 吗？ Can I not go to bed tonight?

Let's learn

02-01

qǐchuáng
起床 get up

shuìjiào
睡觉 sleep, go to bed

zǎoshang
早上 morning

wǎnshang
晚上 night, evening

dào * 到	up to, until 三点到五点，星期一到星期五
ne 呢	(a modal particle) 我是中国人，你呢？
yào 要	to want, would like 你要做什么？我要喝水。

"Pass on the question" game. One student asks a question with "呢", for example "我七点起床，你呢？". Another student answers it and asks his/her neighbor the same question until the whole class finish it. Then start with a new question.

Let's read

02-02

Question:他星期六早上几点起床？

Question:他要做什么？

Pair work. Ask your partner when he/she gets up from Monday to Sunday, and then report.

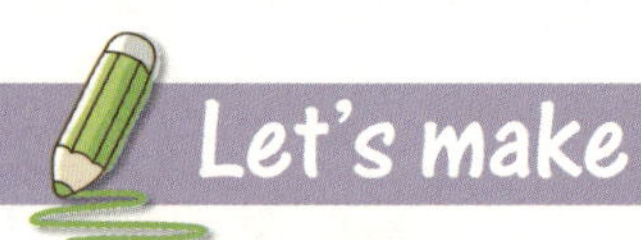

My Schedule

	Xīngqītiān 星期天	Xīngqīyī dào Xīngqīwǔ 星期一到星期五	Xīngqīliù 星期六

Write down the time of each activity in the form according to your daily routine, and then compare with your partner.

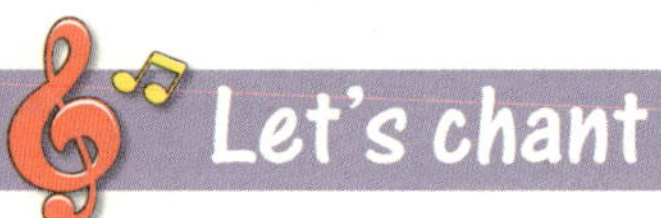

Kuài kuài qǐchuáng, kuài kuài qǐchuáng,
快 快 起床，快 快 起床，

qī diǎn la, qī diǎn la.
7 点 啦，7 点 啦。

Tàiyáng yǐjīng hěn gāo, tàiyáng yǐjīng hěn gāo.
太阳 已经 很 高，太阳 已经 很 高。

Kuài qǐchuáng, kuài qǐchuáng!
快 起床，快 起床！

Kuài kuài shuìjiào, kuài kuài shuìjiào,
快 快 睡觉，快 快 睡觉，

jiǔ diǎn la, jiǔ diǎn la.
9 点 啦，9 点 啦。

Yuèliang yǐjīng hěn gāo, yuèliang yǐjīng hěn gāo.
月亮 已经 很 高，月亮 已经 很 高。

Kuài shuìjiào, kuài shuìjiào!
快 睡觉，快 睡觉！

Nǐ zěnme bù qǐchuáng?
你怎么不 起床？

Read the story and act it out.

1 Listening.  02-05

1.	A	B	C
2.	A	B	C
3.	A	B	C
4.	A	B	C

2 Reading.

A  B  C  D 

5. A: Wǒ wǎnshang jiǔ diǎn shuìjiào, nǐ ne?
我晚上9点睡觉，你呢？
B: Wǒ shí diǎn duō shuìjiào.
我10点多睡觉。 ☐

6. A: Nǐ yào chī píngguǒ ma?
你要吃苹果吗？
B: Bù chī, xièxie!
不吃，谢谢！ ☐

7. A: Nǐ zǎoshang jǐ diǎn qǐchuáng?
你早上几点起床？
B: Qī diǎn.
7点。 ☐

8. A: Nǐ xīngqī jǐ qù Zhōngguó?
你星期几去中国？
B: Xīngqī'èr.
星期二。 ☐

Lesson 3 你的铅笔呢？

Where is your pencil?

Key Sentences

Nǐ de qiānbǐ ne?
- 你的铅笔呢？ Where is your pencil?

Wǒ de shūbāo zài zhuōzi shang.
- 我的 书包 在桌子 上。 My schoolbag is on the table.

03-01

lǐ mian 里（面）	in, inside 在里面；书包里
shàng bian 上（边）	on 在上边；桌子上
ǎi * 矮	short (in height), dwarf 小矮人

Relay game. Each student holds a word card. One student says "铅笔，铅笔，桌子", and then the student who is holding the "桌子" card continues the game.

Questions: 她的铅笔在哪儿？她的书包呢？

Questions: 房间里有什么？没有什么？

1. Ask and answer questions about each other's stuff according to the first text.
2. Describe your classroom according to the second text.

Draw your room and introduce the location of your stuff to your partner.
e.g. 书包在桌子上。

Shàng, xià, zuǒ, yòu,
上，下，左，右，
shàng, xià, zuǒ, yòu,
上，下，左，右，
zài shàngbian, zài xiàbian,
在上边，在下边，
zài zuǒbian, zài yòubian,
在左边，在右边，
xiàng shàng kàn, xiàng xià kàn,
向上看，向下看，
xiàng zuǒ kàn, xiàng yòu kàn.
向左看，向右看。

Mini story

03-04

Zhǎo dōngxi

找 东西

Read the story and act it out.

Test

1 Listening. 03-05

A  B  C  D

1. ☐

2. ☐

3. ☐

4. ☐

2 Reading: True or false.

5.	 kān diànshì 看 电视	6.	 zhuōzi hé yǐzi 桌子 和 椅子
7.	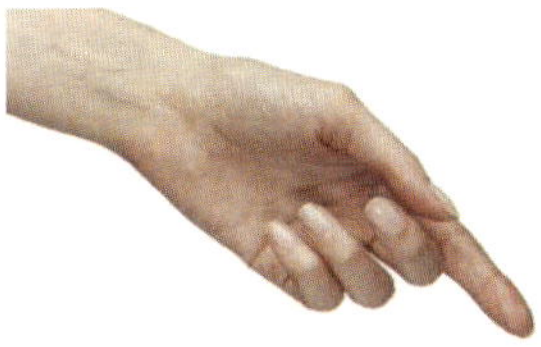 zài shàngbian 在 上边	8.	 zài lǐmian 在 里面

Lesson 4 书包里有两本书。

There are two books in the schoolbag.

Key Sentences

Yì zhī shì lǜsè de.
- 一只是绿色的。 One is green.

Shūbāo li yǒu liǎng běn shū.
- 书包里有 两 本 书。 There are two books in the schoolbag.

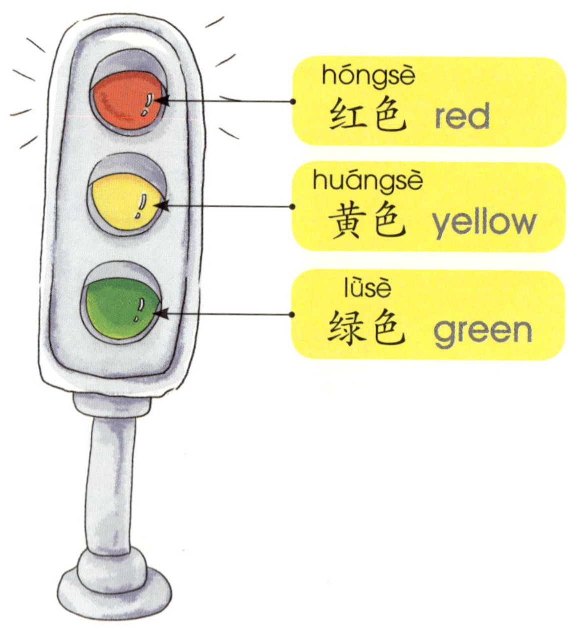

"Touch the color" game. The teacher or a student states a color and the rest of the class compete to touch that flash card.

zhī 只	(a measure word for some animals and some body parts) 一只猫，一只眼睛
míngzi 名字	name 名字叫豆豆
piàoliang 漂亮	beautiful 很漂亮
yánsè 颜色	color 书包是什么颜色的？
liǎng 两	two 两个苹果
běn * 本	(a measure word for books) 两本书

Question: 豆豆的眼睛是什么颜色的？

Question: 书包里有什么？

What color is your schoolbag? What's in it?

Let's color

Pair work. Paint the animals with the color you like, and then check with your partner by using the sentence patterns below:

A：你的……是什么颜色的？

B：我的……是……色的。

Let's play

Group work. Each student takes out stationery and puts them on one desk, and then tells the class who the owner is, item by item.

e.g. 这个铅笔是Emma的。

Guò mǎlù
过马路

"红灯绿灯黄灯" game. A student says one of the words below, and the others do the corresponding action.

绿灯：go slowly 黄灯：go quickly 红灯：stop

Test

1 Listening.  04-04

1.	A	B	C
2.	A	B	C
3.	A	B	C
4.	A	B	C

2 Reading.

huáng A 黄　　liǎng B 两　　piàoliang C 漂亮　　míngzi D 名字

Wǒ yǒu ( ) zhī niǎo, xǐhuan ma?
5. A：我 有（　　）只 鸟，喜欢 吗？

Xǐhuan, zhēn hǎowánr.
B：喜欢，真 好玩儿。

Nà ge rén jiào shénme ( )?
6. A：那 个 人 叫 什么（　　）？

Duìbuqǐ, nǐ shuō shéi?
B：对不起，你 说 谁？

Nǐ de xiǎo māo shì shénme yánsè de?
7. A：你的 小 猫 是 什么 颜色 的？

Wǒ de xiǎo māo shì ( ) sè de.
B：我 的 小 猫 是（　　）色的。

Nǐ de yǎnjing zhēn ( ).
8. A：你的 眼睛 真（　　）。

Shì ma? Xièxie nǐ!
B：是 吗？谢谢 你！

Lesson 5 你会不会做饭？

Can you cook?

Key Sentences

Nǐ huì bu huì zuò fàn?
- 你会不会做饭？ Can you cook?

Nǐ māma shì bu shì chúshī?
- 你妈妈是不是厨师？ Is your mother a chef?

bāozi
包子 baozi

yīshēng
医生 doctor

chúshī
*厨师 chef, cook

huì 会	can 会做饭，不会做包子
zuò 做	to do 做饭
zhēn 真	really, real 真大，真漂亮
hǎochī 好吃	delicious 很好吃，不好吃

"Touch the words" game. All the new words are written on the blackboard. The students touch the words as quickly as possible when the teacher reads them.

Let's read

05-02

1 Jiějie, nǐ huì bu huì zuò fàn?
姐姐，你会不会做饭？

2 Huì. Nǐ yào chī shénme?
会。你要吃什么？

3 Wǒ yào chī bāozi.
我要吃包子。

4 Wǒ bú huì zuò bāozi.
我不会做包子。

Question: 姐姐会不会做包子？

1 Zhè ge bāozi zhēn hǎochī!
这个包子真好吃！

2 Zhè shì wǒ māma zuò de.
这是我妈妈做的。

3 Nǐ māma shì bu shì chúshī?
你妈妈是不是厨师？

4 Bú shì, wǒ māma shì yīshēng.
不是，我妈妈是医生。

Question: 他妈妈是不是医生？

1. Group work. The whole class is divided into two or three groups. When the teacher asks a question with “会不会” or “是不是”, the groups compete to answer the question. See which group will win.
2. Pair work. Tell your partner what your family members' jobs are, and what they can cook.

Let's match

shì bu shì
是不是

huì bu huì
会不会

yào bu yào
要不要

gāo bu gāo
高不高

dà bu dà
大不大

piàoliang bu piàoliang
漂亮不漂亮

① Tā de gèzi
她的个子______？

② Nǐ de shǒu
你的手______？

③ Nǐ zuò fàn?
你______做饭？

④ Nǐ māma
你妈妈______？

⑤ Nǐ hē niúnǎi?
你______喝牛奶？

⑥ Nǐ bàba yīshēng?
你爸爸______医生？

Let's play

Pair work. Play dice, and then ask and answer questions in turn with your partner according to the pictures as the example. No need to answer according to your real situation. Only good grammar is necessary. See which group finish it first.

e.g. A：妈妈会不会做饭？　B：妈妈会做饭。

Chǒuxiǎoyā
丑小鸭

Test

1 Listening.  05-04

A B C D

1. □

2. □

3. □

4. □

2 Reading.

5. Nǐ māma shì zuò shénme de? 你 妈妈 是 做 什么 的？	□	A	Bāozi. 包子。
6. Zhège nǐ yào bu yào? 这个 你 要 不 要？	□	B	Tā bú huì. 她不 会。
7. Nǐ jiějie huì bu huì zuò miàntiáor? 你姐姐会 不 会 做 面条儿？	□	C	Wǒ yào. 我 要。
8. Míngtiān zǎoshang wǒmen chī shénme? 明天 早上 我们 吃 什么？	□	D	Yīshēng. 医生。

Lesson 6

包子多少钱一个？

How much is one *baozi*?

Key Sentences

Bāozi duōshao qián yí ge?
- 包子多少钱一个？ How much is one *baozi*?

Liǎng kuài qián yí ge.
- 两块钱一个。 Two *kuai* for one *baozi*.

06-01

qián
钱 money

chá
茶 tea

mǎi 买	to buy 买包子
duōshao 多少	how much, how many 多少钱，多少本书
kuài 块	*kuai* (a unit for RMB) 两块钱
bēi *杯	cup (a measure word for drinks) 一杯茶
Tài guì le! *太贵了！	It's too expensive!

"Echo" game. The teacher says one word, and the students repeat it several times from loud to a whisper. Then start with a new word.

Question: 三个包子多少钱？

Question: 绿茶多少钱一杯？

Role play. Use the texts above to order something to eat or drink.

Let's know RMB

yí kuài
1 块

wǔ kuài
5 块

shí kuài
10 块

èrshí kuài
20 块

wǔshí kuài
50 块

yìbǎi kuài
100 块

Let's chant

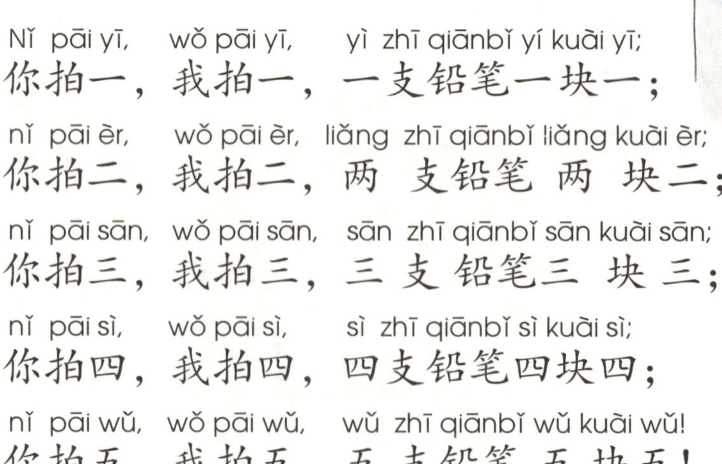

Nǐ pāi yī, wǒ pāi yī, yì zhī qiānbǐ yí kuài yī;
你拍一，我拍一，一支铅笔一块一；
nǐ pāi èr, wǒ pāi èr, liǎng zhī qiānbǐ liǎng kuài èr;
你拍二，我拍二，两支铅笔两块二；
nǐ pāi sān, wǒ pāi sān, sān zhī qiānbǐ sān kuài sān;
你拍三，我拍三，三支铅笔三块三；
nǐ pāi sì, wǒ pāi sì, sì zhī qiānbǐ sì kuài sì;
你拍四，我拍四，四支铅笔四块四；
nǐ pāi wǔ, wǒ pāi wǔ, wǔ zhī qiānbǐ wǔ kuài wǔ!
你拍五，我拍五，五支铅笔五块五！

Mǎi huā
买花

Why are the roses more expensive today?

Test

1 Listening.  06-05

A　　B　　C　　D

1. □

2. □

3. □

4. □

2 Reading.

duōshao　　mǎi　　kuài　　chá
A 多少　　B 买　　C 块　　D 茶

Nǐ　shénme?
5. A：你（　　）什么？

Wǒ mǎi píngguǒ.
B：我 买 苹果。

Xiǎo péngyou, liǎng ge wǔ shì　?
6. A：小 朋友，两 个 5 是（　　）？

Shì shí.
B：是 10。

Zhè ge shūbāo duōshao qián?
7. A：这 个 书包 多少 钱？

Bāshí　.
B：80（　　）。

Qǐng zuò, nǐ hē shénme? Hē　?
8. A：请 坐，你喝 什么？喝（　　）？

Hǎode, xièxie!
B：好的，谢谢！

Lesson 7

今天比昨天热。

Today is hotter than yesterday.

Key Sentences

Běijīng tiānqì zěnmeyàng?
- 北京天气怎么样？ How is the weather in Beijing?

Jīntiān bǐ zuótiān rè.
- 今天比昨天热。 Today is hotter than yesterday.

lěng
冷 cold

rè
热 hot

Běijīng
北京 Beijing

Niǔyuē
*纽约 New York

bīng shuǐ
*冰 水 ice water

Try to think where it is hot and where it is cold now around the world.

tiānqì 天气	weather 天气很好
zěnmeyàng 怎么样	how 天气怎么样？
bǐ 比	than 今天比昨天热。
zuótiān 昨天	yesterday 昨天很热；我昨天去商店了。
juéde 觉得	to feel, to think 觉得很热，觉得很好
hǎohē 好喝	good to drink, drinkable 很好喝

Let's read

07-02

1 Běijīng tiānqì zěnmeyàng?
北京天气怎么样?

2 Hěn hǎo, bù lěng yě bú rè.
很好，不冷也不热。
Niǔyuē ne?
纽约呢?

3 Niǔyuē jīntiān bǐ zuótiān rè.
纽约今天比昨天热。

Question: 纽约今天天气怎么样?

Wǒ xǐhuan hē bīng shuǐ, bàba māma xǐhuan hē rè shuǐ.
我喜欢喝冰水，爸爸妈妈喜欢喝热水。
Wǒ juéde bīng shuǐ bǐ rè shuǐ hǎohē, bàba māma juéde rè shuǐ bǐ bīng shuǐ hǎohē. Tāmen bú rè ma?
我觉得冰水比热水好喝，爸爸妈妈觉得热水比冰水好喝。他们不热吗?

Question: 爸爸觉得热水和冰水哪个好喝?

Introduce your family's favorite drinks according to the second text by using "比".

Pair work. Look at the pictures and answer the question by using the words "热" or "冷".

Jīntiān tiānqì zěnmeyàng?
A：今天天气怎么样？

Jīntiān
B：今天________。

日期 Date			
最高气温 Highest temperature			
最低气温 Lowest temperature			

Record the maximum and minimum air temperature of your city in the next 3 days. Then using "比" to compare.

Tiānqì zěnmeyàng?
天气 怎么样?

Niǔyuē tiānqì zěnmeyàng? Tiānqì zěnmeyàng?
纽约天气 怎么样? 天气怎么样?
Niǔyuē bǐ Běijīng lěng, lěng, lěng, lěng, lěng, lěng.
纽约比北京 冷, 冷, 冷, 冷, 冷, 冷。
Xīní tiānqì zěnmeyàng? Tiānqì zěnmeyàng?
悉尼天气怎么样? 天气怎么样?
Xīní bǐ Běijīng rè, rè, rè, rè, rè, rè.
悉尼比北京热, 热, 热, 热, 热, 热。

Bǐ yi bǐ
比一比

Read the story and act it out.

Test

1 Listening. 07-05

A B C D

1. ☐
2. ☐
3. ☐
4. ☐

2 Reading.

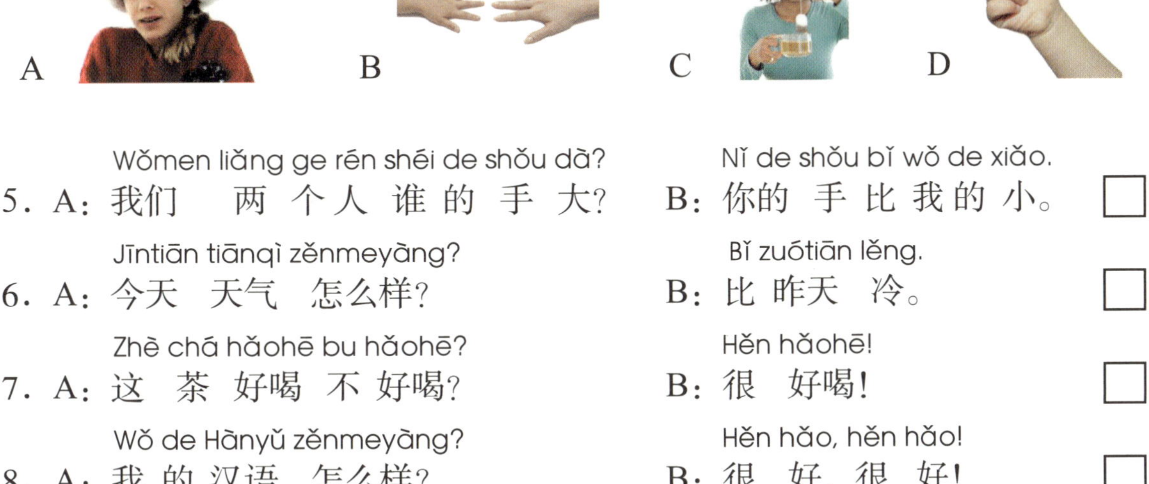

A B C D

5. A：我们 两 个 人 谁 的 手 大？(Wǒmen liǎng ge rén shéi de shǒu dà?)
B：你的 手 比 我 的 小。(Nǐ de shǒu bǐ wǒ de xiǎo.) ☐

6. A：今天 天气 怎么样？(Jīntiān tiānqì zěnmeyàng?)
B：比 昨天 冷。(Bǐ zuótiān lěng.) ☐

7. A：这 茶 好喝 不 好喝？(Zhè chá hǎohē bu hǎohē?)
B：很 好喝！(Hěn hǎohē!) ☐

8. A：我 的 汉语 怎么样？(Wǒ de Hànyǔ zěnmeyàng?)
B：很 好，很 好！(Hěn hǎo, hěn hǎo!) ☐

Lesson 8 马丁比我大三岁。

Martin is three years older than me.

Key Sentences

Tāmen yě shì xiǎoxuéshēng.
- 他们 也是 小学生。They are elementary school students, too.

Mǎdīng bǐ wǒ dà sān suì.
- 马丁 比我大三 岁。Martin is three years older than me.

dìdi
弟弟 little brother

mèimei
妹妹 litter sister

péngyou 朋友	friend 好朋友
tóngxué 同学	classmate 我的同学
yě 也	also, too 我也是学生。
xuésheng 学生	student 小学生

Say as many sentences with "也" as possible.
e.g. 我是学生，弟弟也是学生。

08-02

Gēge bǐ jiějie gāo, jiějie bǐ wǒ gāo, wǒ bǐ dìdi,
哥哥比姐姐高，姐姐比我高，我比弟弟、
mèimei gāo. Wǒmen bǐ Dàhuáng gāo hěn duō.
妹妹高。我们比大黄高很多。

Questions: 谁比他高？他比谁高？

Zhè shì Sūshān, zhè shì Mǎdīng, tāmen shì wǒ de hǎo péngyou.
这是苏珊，这是马丁，他们是我的好朋友。
Sūshān hé Mǎdīng shì tóngxué, yě shì xiǎoxuéshēng. Mǎdīng bǐ
苏珊和马丁是同学，也是小学生。马丁比
wǒ dà sān suì, Sūshān bǐ wǒ dà liǎng suì.
我大三岁，苏珊比我大两岁。

Question: 马丁比苏珊大几岁？

Two students stand together and see who is taller.

Let's say

Describe the pictures by using the pattern "A+比+B+*Adj*.+Number".

Let's write

	我	同桌 my partner
年龄 age		
身高 height		
体重 weight		
鞋的大小 shoe size		

Fill in the form and compare with your partner with the sentence pattern "A+比+B+*Adj*.+Number".

Bǐ gāo ǎi
比高矮

Read the story and act it out.

Test

1 Listening. 08-04

A  B  C  D 

1. □
2. □
3. □
4. □

2 Reading.

A   B  C  D 

	A	B	
5.	Zhè ge rén shì shéi? A：这个人是谁？	Tā shì māma de yí ge hǎo péngyou. B：她是妈妈的一个好朋友。	□
6.	Nǐ rènshi tā ma? A：你认识她吗？	Tā shì wǒ tóngxué. B：她是我同学。	□
7.	Nǐ dìdi duō dà? A：你弟弟多大？	Qī suì, tā bǐ wǒ xiǎo liǎng suì. B：7岁，他比我小两岁。	□
8.	Nǐmen shéi gāo? A：你们谁高？	Tā bǐ wǒ gāo hěn duō. B：他比我高很多。	□

Lesson 9

你今天做什么了？

What did you do today?

Key Sentences

Wǒ chīle yí ge píngguǒ hé yí ge xiāngjiāo.
- 我吃了一个苹果和一个香蕉。 I ate an apple and a banana.

Wǒ méi huà xióngmāo.
- 我没画熊猫。 I didn't draw a panda.

Let's learn

09-01

xiāngjiāo
香蕉 banana

xióngmāo
熊猫 panda

shuǐguǒ * 水果	fruit 吃水果，很多水果
le 了	(perfective particle) 你吃什么了？
huà 画	to draw, to paint; picture, drawing 画小鸟，画画儿
méi yǒu 没（有）	didn't (do), haven't (done) 我没吃香蕉。

List fruit and animals in Chinese first. Then use them to make phrases with "吃" and "画". Say the phrases one by one. (The same phrase can't be used twice.)

Let's read

09-02

Question:她吃了什么水果？

Question:他画熊猫了吗？

"Antonyms" game. One student says a sentence, e.g. "我吃苹果了", and the other says the opposite, e.g. "我没吃苹果".

Let's color

09-03

Please color in the animals according to the recording.

Replace it with other food or fruit.

Rúguǒ chīle xiāngjiāo nǐ jiù pāi pāi shǒu,
如果吃了 香蕉 你就拍拍手，

Rúguǒ méi chī xiāngjiāo nǐ jiù duò duò jiǎo,
如果没吃 香蕉 你就跺跺脚，

Rúguǒ chīle xiāngjiāo nǐ jiù pāi pāi shǒu, pāi pāi shǒu,
如果吃了 香蕉 你就拍拍手，拍拍手，

Rúguǒ méi chī xiāngjiāo nǐ jiù duò duò jiǎo.
如果没吃 香蕉 你就跺跺脚。

Kàn yīshēng
看 医生

Read the story and act it out.

Test

1 Listening: True or false.  09-06

1.		
2.		
3.		
4.		

2 Reading.

Nǐ zuótiān mǎi shénme le? 5. 你 昨天 买 什么 了？	☐	Méi qǐchuáng. A 没 起床。
Nǐ gēge qǐchuáng le ma? 6. 你 哥哥 起床 了 吗？	☐	Liǎng ge. B 两 个。
Nǐ chīfàn le ma? 7. 你 吃饭 了 吗？	☐	Píngguǒ. C 苹果。
Nǐ chīle jǐ ge xiāngjiāo? 8. 你吃了几个 香蕉？	☐	Chī le. D 吃 了。

Lesson 10 你怎么了？

What's wrong with you?

Key Sentences

Nǐ zěnme le?
- 你怎么了？ What's wrong with you?

Xiànzài wǒ shǒu bù téng le.
- 现在 我 手 不 疼 了。 My hand doesn't hurt now.

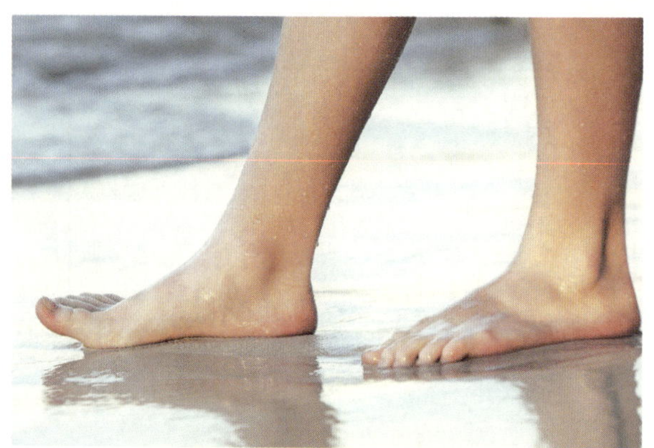

jiǎo
脚 foot

yīyuàn
医院 hospital

zěnme le 怎么了	what's wrong with… 手怎么了？
téng * 疼	painful 很疼，不疼

The whole class name the body parts in Chinese first. Then one student asks "你怎么了", and the other answers the question while acting it out.

10-02

Question: 明明怎么了？

Question: 明明为什么不去医院？

Role play. One student acts as the mother and the other as the child. Make a dialogue according to the texts.

Let's match

1. 

2. 

3. 

4.  

Jiā li méiyǒu niúnǎi le.
A. 家里没有牛奶了。

Wǒ bù chī le.
B. 我不吃了。

Wǒ jiǎo bù téng le.
C. 我脚不疼了。

Wǒ míngtiān bú qù xuéxiào le.
D. 我明天不去学校了。

Let's imagine

1. 

2. 

3. 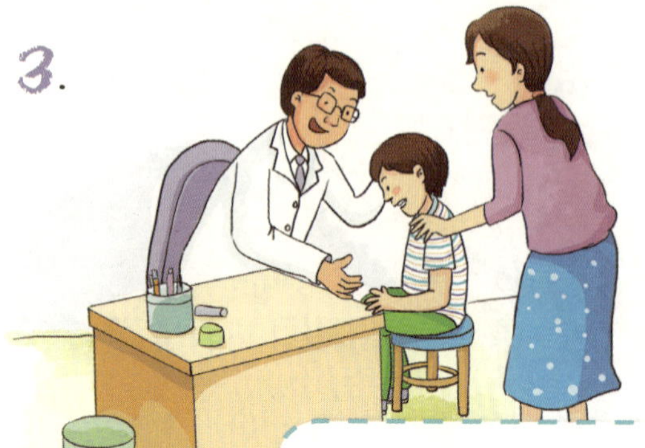

Group work. In groups of three, imagine the end of the story. Then act out the whole story. See which story is the most interesting.

Hǎo péngyou
好朋友

Read the story and act it out.

Test

1 Listening.  10-04

1.	A	B	C
2.	A	B	C
3.	A	B	C
4.	A	B	C

2 Reading.

A zěnme 怎么　　B bù 不　　C le 了　　D kěyǐ 可以

5. A: Māma, jiāli méiyǒu niúnǎi ( ).　B: Wǒ míngtiān qù mǎi.
   A：妈妈，家里没有牛奶（　　）。　B：我明天去买。

6. A: Qǐng hē chá.　B: ( ) hē le, wǒ xiànzài yào qù xuéxiào.
   A：请喝茶。　B：（　　）喝了，我现在要去学校。

7. A: Jiějie, nǐ de shǒu ( ) le?　B: Méi guānxi.
   A：姐姐，你的手（　　）了？　B：没关系。

8. A: Jīntiān zhōngwǔ chī mǐfàn, ( ) ma?
   A：今天中午吃米饭，（　　）吗？
   B: Kěyǐ.
   B：可以。

Lesson 11 我来北京一年了。

I've been in Beijing for one year.

Key Sentences

Sān diǎn líng wǔ le.
- 三点零五了。 It's five past three.

Wǒ lái Běijīng yì nián le.
- 我来北京一年了。 I've been in Beijing for one year.

líng 零	zero 三点零五，六零七房间
wán 玩	to play 玩十分钟，去朋友家玩
fēnzhōng 分钟	minute 十分钟
lái 来	to come 来北京，来学校
nián 年	year 一年
xuéxí 学习	to study 学习汉语
Hànyǔ 汉语	Chinese 汉语名字，说汉语
yòng * 用	to use 用汉语，用铅笔写字
dǎ diànhuà 打电话	to make a phone call
yǐqián * 以前	before, previously 一年以前

"Shout and whisper" game. When the teacher shouts a word, the students whisper; when the teacher whispers a word, the students shout.

Let's read

11-02

Question:现在几点了？

Question:她现在会做什么了？

Tell your partner about your changes since you began to study Chinese, and then tell the whole class.

Let's draw

Pair work. Draw the time on the clock, and then tell your partner the time in Chinese.

Let's describe

Pair work. Describe the changes of "my cat" with your partner according to the pictures.

Mini story

11-03

Wǒ de Xīngqītiān
我的星期天

1

Zǎoshang, wǒ hé bàba yùndòng
早上，我和爸爸运动

liǎng ge xiǎoshí.
两个小时。

2

Zhōngwǔ, wǒ shuì yí ge xiǎoshí.
中午，我睡一个小时。

3

Xiàwǔ, wǒ kàn yí ge xiǎoshí diànshì.
下午，我看一个小时电视。

4

Wǎnshang, wǒ kàn bàn ge xiǎoshí shū.
晚上，我看半个小时书。

What's your daily routine? Tell your partner.

1 Listening.

11-04

1\. A zàijiàn 再见　B Xīngqīyī 星期一　C liǎng diǎn líng qī 两 点 零 七

2\. A jǐ ge yǐzi 几个椅子　B bú kèqi 不客气　C kěyǐ 可以

3\. A bā fēnzhōng 八 分钟　B dǎ diànhuà 打 电话　C lái Běijīng 来北京

4\. A tā zài liù líng qī 他在六零七　B tā zài fángjiān li 他在 房间 里　C tā jīnnián bā suì le 他 今年 八岁了

2 Reading.

A 

B 

C 

D 

5\. A: Xiànzài jǐ diǎn le? 现在 几 点 了？
B: Jiǔ diǎn. 九 点。 ☐

6\. A: Wǒ de tóufa cháng ma? 我 的 头发 长 吗？
B: Hěn cháng. 很 长。 ☐

7\. A: Nǐ huì yòng Hànyǔ dǎ diànhuà ma? 你 会 用 汉语 打 电话 吗？
B: Huì. 会。 ☐

8\. A: Shéi de gèzi gāo? 谁 的 个子 高？
B: Jiějie de gèzi bǐ dìdi gāo. 姐姐 的 个子 比 弟弟 高。 ☐

Lesson 12 复习 Review

1 Bingo. Name the pictures in Chinese with your partner, and then put the numbers in the box randomly. The teacher says the words and the students circle the right one. Shout "Bingo" when you get 3 in a row.

2 Please find the missing words for the sentences from the word box on the right.

1	Wǒ chī ______ liǎng ge dà píngguǒ. 我吃______两个大苹果。
2	Gēge ______ wǒ gāo hěn duō. 哥哥______我高很多。
3	Zuótiān shì Xīngqīliù, wǒ ______ qù xuéxiào. 昨天是星期六，我______去学校。
4	Jiějie de tóufa cháng ______. 姐姐的头发长______。
5	Qǐng ______ yào shuōhuà. 请______要说话。
6	Jīntiān tiānqì ______ rè! 今天天气______热！

3 Pair work. One student asks a question with the word given, and the other answers it according to the picture.

huì
会

diǎn
点

bǐ
比

qián
钱

le
了

zài
在

4 Read the passage, and circle the picture which is not true.

Nǐ kàn, zhè zhī xiǎo huáng māo shì wǒ de hǎo péngyou, tā de míngzi jiào Xiǎohuáng.
你看，这只小黄猫是我的好朋友，它的名字叫小黄。
Xiǎohuáng báitiān shuìjiào, wǎnshang bú shuìjiào. Tā bù xǐhuan chī yú, xǐhuan hē nǎi.
小黄白天睡觉，晚上不睡觉。它不喜欢吃鱼，喜欢喝奶。
Xiǎohuáng xiànzài yí ge yuè le, bǐ wǒ de xié dà le.
小黄现在一个月了，比我的鞋大了。

1

2

3

4

词语表 Vocabulary

A

* 矮	short, dwarf	ǎi	13

B

包子	*baozi*	bāozi	23
* 杯	cup(a measure word for drinks)	bēi	28
北京	Beijing	Běijīng	33
* 本	(a measure word for books)	běn	18
比	than	bǐ	33
* 冰水	ice water	bīng shuǐ	33
不客气	You're welcome.	bú kèqi	3
不要	don't	bú yào	3

C

茶	tea	chá	28
* 厨师	chef, cook	chúshī	23
* 床	bed	chuáng	13

D

打电话	to make a phone call	dǎ diànhuà	53
* 到	up to, until	dào	8
弟弟	little brother	dìdi	38
电视	television	diànshì	13
对不起	I'm sorry.	duìbuqǐ	3
多少	how much, how many	duōshao	28

F

房间	room	fángjiān	13
分钟	minute	fēnzhōng	53

H

汉语	Chinese	Hànyǔ	53
好吃	delicious	hǎochī	23
好喝	good to drink, drinkable	hǎohē	33
红色	red	hóngsè	18
画	to draw, to paint; picture, drawing	huà	43
黄色	yellow	huángsè	18
会	can	huì	23

J

脚	foot	jiǎo	48
觉得	to feel, to think	juéde	33

K

可以	may	kěyǐ	3
块	*kuai* (a unit for RMB)	kuài	28

L

来	to come	lái	53
了	(perfective particle)	le	43
冷	cold	lěng	33
里(面)	in, inside	lǐ (mian)	13
两	two	liǎng	18
零	zero	líng	53
绿色	green	lǜsè	18

M

买	to buy	mǎi	28
没(有)	didn't (do), haven't (done)	méi (yǒu)	43
没关系	Never mind.	méi guānxi	3
妹妹	little sister	mèimei	38
名字	name	míngzi	18

N

呢	(a modal particle)	ne	8
年	year	nián	53
* 纽约	New York	Niǔyuē	33

P

朋友	friend	péngyou	38
漂亮	beautiful	piàoliang	18

Q

起床	get up	qǐchuáng	8
铅笔	pencil	qiānbǐ	13
钱	money	qián	28
请	please	qǐng	3

R

热	hot	rè	33

S

上(边)	on	shàng (bian)	13
书包	schoolbag	shūbāo	13
* 水果	fruit	shuǐguǒ	43
睡觉	sleep, go to bed	shuìjiào	8
说话	to talk, to speak	shuōhuà	3

T

* 太贵了!	It's too expensive!	Tài guì le!	28
* 疼	painful	téng	48
天气	weather	tiānqì	33
同学	classmate	tóngxué	38

W

玩	to play	wán	53

晚上	night, evening	wǎnshang	8

X

香蕉	banana	xiāngjiāo	43
熊猫	panda	xióngmāo	43
学生	student	xuésheng	38
学习	to study	xuéxí	53

Y

颜色	color	yánsè	18
要	to want, would like	yào	8
也	also, too	yě	38
医生	doctor	yīshēng	23
医院	hospital	yīyuàn	48
* 以前	before, previously	yǐqián	53
椅子	chair	yǐzi	13
* 用	to use	yòng	53

Z

早上	morning	zǎoshang	8
怎么了	what's wrong with...	zěnme le	48
怎么样	how	zěnmeyàng	33
真	really, real	zhēn	23
只	(a measure word for some animals and some body parts)	zhī	18
桌子	table	zhuōzi	13
昨天	yesterday	zuótiān	33
坐	to sit	zuò	3
做	to do	zuò	23

课文和小故事翻译
Text and Mini Story Translation

Lesson 1　Let's read

Boy: How are you? May I sit here?
Girl: Yes. Have a seat, please.
Boy: Thank you!
Girl: You're welcome.

Girl: Please don't talk.
Two boys: OK. Sorry.
Girl: It doesn't matter.

Lesson 1　Mini story

Cinderella

① Cinderella: Can I go?
Stepmother/Sisters: No.
② Cinderella: Can I wear it?
Fairy: Yes.
Cinderella: Thank you!
③ Prince: Can I ask you to dance?
Cinderella: Yes.
④ Prince: Where are you going?

Lesson 2　Let's read

Boy A: What time do you get up every morning?
Boy B: I get up at 7 o'clock from Monday to Friday.
Boy A: What about Saturday and Sunday?
Boy B: I get up at 12 o'clock on Saturday and Sunday.

Kid: Mom, can I not go to bed tonight?
Mom: What do you want to do?
Kid: I'd like to see at what time the fish goes to sleep.

Lesson 2　Mini story

Why don't you get up?

① Little squirrel: Mom, I'd like to go out and play with my friends!
Mom: OK.
② Little squirrel: Where are you? Come out and play!
③ Little squirrel: Brother bear, why don't you get up today?
④ Little squirrel: Brother frog, why don't you get up today?
⑤ Little squirrel: Why don't they get up today?
Grandpa goat: In winter they sleep all day and never get up.

Lesson 3　Let's read

Little brother: Sister, where's is your pencil?
Big sister: It is in my schoolbag.
Little brother: Where's is your schoolbag?
Big sister: On the table.

Snow White: Look, this is the room of the seven dwarves. Inside there are little beds, little tables and little chairs.
Kids: Where's the TV?
Snow White: There is no TV in the room.

Lesson 3　Mini story

Looking for something

① Kid: Mom, where's my pencil?
Mom: In the schoolbag.
② Kid: Where's my schoolbag?
Mom: On the chair.
③ Dad: Where's my wallet?
Mom: In the room.
④ Dad: Where are my glasses?
Mom: On your nose.

Lesson 4　Let's read

I have a cat named Doudou. Doudou has very beautiful eyes, a green one and a yellow one. Doudou really likes to eat fish.

Administrator: What color is your schoolbag?
Kid: Red.
Administrator: What's in your schoolbag?
Kid: Two books.

Lesson 4　Mini story

Crossing the road
① Ducks: One two one; one two one.
② Duckling: Mom, can we cross the road now?
Mom: The light is green. We can cross the road now.
③ Duckling: Can we cross the road now?
Mom: The light is yellow. Quick! Quick!
④ Duckling: Can we cross the road now?
Mom: The light is red. We cannot cross the road now.

Lesson 5　Let's read

Little brother: Sister, can you cook?
Big sister: Yes, I can. What do you want to eat?
Little brother: I want to eat *baozi*.
Big sister: I don't know how to make *baozi*.

Girl: This *baozi* is so tasty!
Boy: My mom made it.
Girl: Is your mother a chef?
Boy: No, my mother is a doctor.

Lesson 5　Mini story

Ugly Duckling
① Father duck: Is your little sister beautiful?
Baby duck: No, she isn't.
② Duck A: Do you like your little sister?
Duck B: No, I don't. She is ugly.
③ Ugly Duckling: Mom, do you love me?
Mother duck: Mom loves you.
④ Ugly Duckling: Mom, I have no friends.
⑤ Ugly Duckling: It's too cold, too cold!
⑥ Swan: Can you fly?
Ugly Duckling: Let me try...

Lesson 6　Let's read

Salesperson: Can I help you?
Kid: How much is one *baozi*?
Salesperson: Two *kuai* for one, and five *kuai* for three.
Kid: I want three. Thanks!

Man: Do you have green tea?
Waitress: Yes.
Man: How much for one glass?
Waitress: 50 *kuai*.
Man: 50 *kuai*?! It's too expensive!

Lesson 6　Mini story

Buying flowers
① Salesperson: How are you? Can I help you?
② Man: How much for one rose?
Salesperson: 10 *kuai*.
③ Man: It's too expensive! Wasn't it 5 *kuai* yesterday?
Salesperson: Yes. Yesterday was February 13th, while today is February 14th.

Lesson 7　Let's read

Friend: How is the weather in Beijing now?
David: It is good, neither cold nor hot. What about New York?
Friend: New York is hotter today than yesterday.

I like to drink ice water. My Mom and Dad like to drink hot water. I think ice water is better than hot water, while my Mom and Dad think hot water is better than ice water. Don't they feel hot?

Lesson 7　Mini story

Let's compare

① Little sister: My big brother is cleverer than me.

② Little sister: My big sister is more beautiful than me.

③ Little sister: I am neither clever nor beautiful.

④ Big brother and sister: You are very cute. We love you!

Lesson 8　Let's read

My big brother is taller than my big sister. Big sister is taller than me. I am taller than my little brother and sister. We are all much taller than Da Huang.

This is Susan, and this is Martin. They are my good friends. Susan and Martin are classmates, and they are also pupils. Martin is 3 years older than me, while Susan is 2 years older than me.

Lesson 8　Mini story

Compare heights

① Camel: I am taller than you, haha.
Goat: ...

② Camel: I am much taller than you, haha.
Goat: ...

③ Goat: I am shorter than you.
Camel: ...

④ Goat: I am shorter than you. But I can also do a lot of things.

Lesson 9　Let's read

Mom: Have you eaten any fruit today?

Daughter: Yes, I have.

Mom: What fruit did you have?

Daughter: I ate an apple and a banana.

Dad: What did you do today?

Son: I did some drawing.

Dad: This panda is so beautiful!

Son: Dad, I didn't draw a panda. This is a puppy!

Lesson 9　Mini story

Seeing the doctor

① Doctor rabbit: What did you eat today?
Little rat: I ate a lot of things.

② Doctor rabbit: What did you eat?
Little rat: I ate a banana, two apples and ice cream.

③ Doctor rabbit: How many ice creams did you have?
Little rat: Three.

④ Doctor rabbit: What else did you have?
Little rat: I also drank four glasses of ice water.

Lesson 10　Let's read

Mom: Mingming, get up!

Mingming: Mom, can I not go to school today?

Mom: What's the matter?

Mingming: My feet hurt!

Mom: Let's go to see the doctor.

Mingming: Mom, I don't want to go to hospital. I will go to school.

Mom: Go to school? Don't your feet hurt?

Mingming: Not anymore!

Lesson 10　Mini story

Good friends

① Little butterfly: How are you!
Little bee/ Little ant: Who are you? We don't know you!

② Little butterfly: I used to be a caterpillar. Now I am a little butterfly!

③ Little bee: You can fly!
Little ant: You are more beautiful than before!

④ Little butterfly: We used to be good friends before. Now we are still good friends!

Lesson 11 Let's read

Son: Mom, what time is it?
Mom: It's five past three.
Son: Can I go over there and play for ten minutes?
Mom: Yes, you can.

I have been in Beijing with my Dad and Mom for one year. I like to study Chinese. Now I can make telephone calls in Chinese. I have grown taller and my hair is longer. My friends say that I am more beautiful than before!

Lesson 11 Mini story

My Sunday

① In the morning, dad and I did physical exercises for 2 hours.

② At noon, I sleep for an hour.

③ In the afternoon, I watch TV for an hour.

④ In the evening, I read books for half an hour.

测试页听力文本
Test Listening Scripts

Lesson 1

1. 请坐。
2. 谢谢妈妈。
3. 请不要说话。
4. 今天吃面条，可以吗？

Lesson 2

1. A: 你明天几点去学校？
   B: 9点。
2. A: 今天晚上我们吃什么？
   B: 吃米饭可以吗？
3. A: 再见！
   B: 再见！我们星期四见！
4. A: 爸爸，星期一我可以不去学校吗？
   B: 不可以。

Lesson 3

1. 这里面没有苹果。
2. 我的书在书包里。
3. 我弟弟有很多铅笔。
4. 猫在桌子上。

Lesson 4

1. A: 你有绿色的铅笔吗？
   B: 有，这儿有。
2. A: 你喜欢哪个椅子？
   B: 我喜欢红色的那个。
3. A: 我的铅笔在这儿。
   B: 有绿色的吗？
4. A: 你要什么颜色的？
   B: 我要黄色的那个。

Lesson 5

1. 妈妈，你的个子真高！
2. 今天的饭不好吃。
3. 我爱做饭。
4. 你看，这个苹果大不大？

Lesson 6

1. A: 喝茶吗？
   B: 好的，谢谢你。
2. A: 我要买那个绿的。
   B: 那个红的也很好。
3. A: 姐姐，我们有几块钱？
   B: 5块。
4. A: 那是多少钱？
   B: 我看看，一块、两块……

Lesson 7

1. 妹妹爱喝热牛奶。
2. 爸爸的个子比我高。
3. 你看，我的书包怎么样？
4. 你觉得这儿的面条儿好吃不好吃？

Lesson 8

1. 你弟弟几岁？
2. 这儿有四个学生。
3. 我们两个人是好朋友。
4. 我的个子比你高。

Lesson 9

1. 两只大熊猫
2. 没睡觉
3. 吃香蕉
4. 画画儿

Lesson 10

1. A: 你姐姐去哪儿了？
   B: 她去医院了。
2. A: 你的脚怎么样了？
   B: 好多了，谢谢你。
3. A: 医生，我的耳朵好了吗？
   B: 我看看。
4. A: 他怎么了？
   B: 没关系，他觉得不好吃。

Lesson 11

1. 现在几点了？
   A 再见
   B 星期一
   C 两点零七
2. 我可以玩十分钟吗？
   A 几个椅子
   B 不客气
   C 可以
3. 你在做什么呢？
   A 八分钟
   B 打电话
   C 来北京
4. 你弟弟在哪个房间？
   A 他在六零七
   B 他在房间里
   C 他今年八岁了

测试页答案
Test Answers

Lesson 1

1. × 2. √ 3. √ 4. ×

5. C 6. A 7. D 8. B

Lesson 2

1. B 2. C 3. B 4. B

5. D 6. B 7. A 8. C

Lesson 3

1. B 2. C 3. A 4. D

5. × 6. √ 7. × 8. √

Lesson 4

1. C 2. B 3. A 4. C

5. B 6. D 7. A 8. C

Lesson 5

1. C 2. A 3. B 4. D

5. D 6. C 7. B 8. A

Lesson 6

1. B 2. D 3. C 4. A

5. B 6. A 7. C 8. D

Lesson 7

1. B 2. A 3. D 4. C

5. B 6. A 7. C 8. D

Lesson 8

1. A 2. D 3. C 4. B

5. D 6. A 7. B 8. C

Lesson 9

1. × 2. √ 3. √ 4. √

5. C 6. A 7. D 8. B

Lesson 10

1. C 2. A 3. B 4. A

5. C 6. B 7. A 8. D

Lesson 11

1. C 2. C 3. B 4. A

5. A 6. D 7. B 8. C

YCT 奖状

__________同学：

恭喜你学完《YCT标准教程2》，表现优秀，特颁此奖状表示鼓励。

教师签名：__________

日期：__________

This award is presented to

____

For an outstanding performance while studying *YCT Standard Course 2*.

Teacher:______________

Date:________________

图书在版编目（CIP）数据

YCT 标准教程．2/ 苏英霞主编；王蕾编．-- 北京 ：
高等教育出版社，2016.3（2026.2重印）
ISBN 978-7-04-044167-3

Ⅰ．①Y… Ⅱ．①苏… ②王… Ⅲ．①汉语－对外汉语
教学－水平考试－教材 Ⅳ．①H195.4

中国版本图书馆CIP数据核字(2015)第306506号

策划编辑 金飞飞　　责任编辑 李 玮　　封面设计 冰河时代　　版式设计 冰河时代
插图绘制 冰河时代　　责任校对 李 玮　　责任印制 刘弘远

出版发行 高等教育出版社
社　　址 北京市西城区德外大街4号
邮政编码 100120
印　　刷 天津鑫丰华印务有限公司
开　　本 889mm×1194mm 1/16
印　　张 5
字　　数 63千字
购书热线 010-58581118
咨询电话 400-810-0598

网　　址 http://morefunchinese.hep.com.cn
http://www.hep.com.cn
网上订购 http://www.hepmall.com.cn
http://www.hepmall.com
http://www.hepmall.cn

版　　次 2016年 3月第1版
印　　次 2026年 2月第 14 次印刷
定　　价 65.00元

物 料 号 44167-A0